THE ALIEN ENIGMA: A GLOBAL PERSPECTIVE ON EXTRATERRESTRIAL ENCOUNTERS

Emma McCarthy

This book is dedicated to my beloved husband, Harry, whose unwavering support, love, and curiosity have been my constant inspiration. Thank you for always believing in me, for sharing in my passion for the unknown, and for being my partner on this incredible journey. This book would not have been possible without you.

CONTENTS

Introduction: The Universal Question

For as long as humanity has looked up at the night sky, we've asked one fundamental question: Are we alone? This question isn't just about the possibility of extraterrestrial life—it's about our place in the cosmos. From the ancient Sumerians to modern-day scientists, we've been captivated by the idea that there might be other beings out there, watching us, or perhaps even interacting with us.

But what if the answer isn't just theoretical? What if we've already encountered these beings? In this book, we're going to explore that very possibility, taking a journey through history, across cultures, and into the personal stories of those who claim to have had contact with something beyond our world. This isn't just about wild speculation or conspiracy theories. Instead, we'll examine real accounts, government documents, and scientific theories, all with an open mind.

The goal isn't to convince you of any one truth but to present the evidence and let you draw your own conclusions. Whether you're a sceptic, a believer, or just curious, this book offers something for everyone. We'll dig into the most famous cases of UFO sightings and alien abductions, but we'll also explore lesser-known stories that challenge our understanding of reality.

As we embark on this journey, I want you to imagine that we're sitting together, perhaps over a cup of coffee, just chatting about the strange and mysterious. I'll share with you the stories I've come across, the research I've done, and the questions that keep me up at night. You might find yourself nodding along, questioning everything, or even feeling a little uneasy. And that's okay. The universe is vast, and the unknown is, by its very nature, unsettling.

But that's what makes it so intriguing. So, let's start by acknowledging the simple truth: We don't know everything. Our understanding of the universe is constantly evolving, and with each new discovery, the line between science fiction and science fact becomes a little blurrier. Could it be that some of the things we've dismissed as fantasy are actually real? Could there be more to the UFO sightings, the abduction stories, and the government cover-ups than we've been led to believe?

In the chapters that follow, we'll explore these questions and more. We'll look at ancient records that suggest humans may have been interacting with otherworldly beings for millennia. We'll dive into the modern UFO phenomenon, dissecting some of the most compelling cases and the government's response to them. We'll listen to the stories of those who claim to have been abducted and try to understand their experiences. And we'll examine the scientific search for extraterrestrial life, considering what it means for us if we're not alone.

This book isn't just a collection of stories and theories—it's an invitation to explore one of the greatest mysteries of our time. Are we alone in the universe? And if not, what does that mean for us, for our future, and for our understanding of reality?

I don't have all the answers, and I don't pretend to. But together, we can explore the evidence, consider the possibilities, and maybe, just maybe, get a little closer to the truth. So, let's begin this journey into the unknown, with an open mind and a sense of curiosity. After all, the truth might be stranger than we ever imagined.

CHAPTER 1: THE HISTORICAL ROOTS OF ALIEN ENCOUNTERS

When we think of alien encounters, our minds often jump to modern UFO sightings, strange lights in the sky, or tales of abductions. But what if I told you that stories of contact with beings from the stars date back thousands of years? In this chapter, we're going to take a journey into the past, exploring ancient texts, artifacts, and legends that some believe point to early interactions with extraterrestrial visitors.

Now, I want to be clear: interpreting ancient history through the lens of modern UFO sightings is controversial, to say the least. Scholars often caution against reading too much into ancient myths or assuming that ancient peoples had the same concepts of "aliens" that we do today. However, when you start looking at the evidence, some of it is hard to ignore.

The Dogon Tribe and the Sirius Mystery

Let's start with one of the most intriguing examples: the Dogon tribe of West Africa. The Dogon have long been known for their complex cosmology, which includes detailed knowledge of the Sirius star system—knowledge that, by all accounts, they shouldn't have had. According to their oral traditions, the Dogon were visited by beings called the Nommo, who came from Sirius B, a star that is invisible to the naked eye and was only confirmed by modern astronomers in the 20th century.

The Dogon's detailed knowledge of Sirius B, including its orbit and density, has baffled researchers for decades. How could an ancient people know so much about a star that is impossible to see without advanced telescopes? Some suggest that the Dogon's knowledge came from contact with extraterrestrial beings, while others argue it could have been passed down from an ancient civilization or through early contact with European explorers. Regardless of the explanation, the Dogon's story raises intriguing questions about what ancient peoples might have known—and how they knew it.

The Nazca Lines: Messages for the Gods or Landing Strips for Aliens?

Next, let's travel to South America, where we find one of the most mysterious ancient sites on Earth: the Nazca Lines of Peru. These massive geoglyphs, which depict various animals, plants, and geometric shapes, are etched into the desert floor and are only fully visible from the air. The question that has puzzled archaeologists and researchers for years is: Why were they made, and who were they meant for?

Some believe that the Nazca Lines were created as messages or offerings to the gods, intended to be seen from the heavens. But others have a different theory. They suggest that the lines were created as landing strips or guides for extraterrestrial spacecraft. The idea might sound far-fetched, but when you consider the precision and scale of the lines—some of which stretch for miles —it's easy to see why this theory has captured the imagination of many.

Of course, mainstream archaeology has its own explanations, ranging from astronomical alignments to ritualistic purposes. But the question remains: Why create something that can only be fully appreciated from above? And who—or what—were the Nazca people trying to communicate with?

Ancient Cave Paintings: Early Artistic Expressions or Encounters with the Unknown?

Our journey now takes us even further back in time, to the caves of prehistoric humans. Around the world, ancient cave paintings depict strange beings, some of which resemble modern descriptions of aliens. In the caves of Tassili n'Ajjer in Algeria, for example, there are depictions of humanoid figures with large, round heads, often interpreted as helmets or space suits. These images, created thousands of years ago, have led some to wonder whether early humans might have encountered visitors from another world.

These cave paintings aren't isolated incidents. Similar depictions have been found in Australia, India, and Europe, all showing figures that seem out of place among the more recognizable animals and humans. While sceptics argue that these figures could represent shamans or gods, the resemblance to modern "grey" aliens is striking.

It's worth considering the possibility that these ancient artists were documenting something they had seen with their own eyes—something that they struggled to understand, just as we do today. Whether these figures represent visitors from another planet or something else entirely, they add another layer of mystery to the question of ancient alien contact.

Theories of Ancient Astronauts: A Controversial Perspective

No discussion of ancient alien encounters would be complete without touching on the controversial theory of ancient astronauts. Popularized by authors like Erich von Däniken, this theory suggests that many ancient civilizations, including the Egyptians, Sumerians, and Mayans, were influenced—or even guided—by extraterrestrial beings. According to this theory, the gods of these civilizations were actually aliens who shared knowledge, technology, and perhaps even their DNA with early humans.

Von Däniken's books, such as *Chariots of the Gods?*, have been both influential and divisive. Critics accuse him of distorting historical facts and underestimating the ingenuity of ancient peoples. However, his ideas have resonated with millions, inspiring a new way of thinking about our past and our place in the universe.

Proponents of the ancient astronaut theory point to the pyramids of Egypt, the megaliths of Stonehenge, and the statues of Easter Island as evidence of advanced technology that ancient humans could not have created on their own. They argue that these structures, along with the myths and legends of gods descending from the sky, suggest a much deeper connection between ancient humans and extraterrestrial beings.

Conclusion: What Does the Past Tell Us About the Present?

As we look back at these ancient stories, artifacts, and structures, we're left with more questions than answers. Were these civilizations really in contact with beings from another world? Or are we simply projecting our modern ideas onto the past? The truth is, we may never know for sure. But what these stories do show us is that the idea of contact with otherworldly beings is not new—it's a thread that runs through the fabric of human history.

In the next chapter, we'll move from the distant past to the present day, exploring the modern UFO phenomenon and how it has captured the imagination of people around the world. But as we do, let's keep in mind the lessons of the past: that the unknown has always fascinated us, and that the line between myth and reality is often thinner than we think.

CHAPTER 2: THE MODERN UFO PHENOMENON

If ancient myths and artifacts hint at early contact with extraterrestrial beings, the 20th and 21st centuries have seen the question of alien life move from whispers and speculation to the forefront of public consciousness. The modern UFO phenomenon is a global one, sparking intense debate, government investigations, and a pop culture explosion. In this chapter, we'll delve into some of the most famous UFO sightings, the government's response to them, and how these incidents have shaped our collective imagination.

The Roswell Incident: What Really Happened?

We can't talk about UFOs without starting with the most infamous case of them all: the Roswell Incident. In July 1947, something crashed in the New Mexico desert near the town of Roswell. The U.S. military quickly recovered the debris and initially reported it as a "flying disc." However, within days, they retracted that statement, claiming the object was merely a weather balloon. But by then, the story had already captured the public's imagination.

Over the years, Roswell has become synonymous with UFOs and government cover-ups. Eyewitnesses came forward with stories of strange materials, bodies of non-human beings, and threats from the military to keep quiet. The official explanation has changed multiple times, with the U.S. government eventually admitting in the 1990s that the object was part of a top-secret project aimed at detecting Soviet nuclear tests.

Despite these explanations, many still believe that what crashed at Roswell was not of this Earth. The event has inspired countless books, documentaries, and even a museum dedicated to the incident. Roswell represents the point where UFOs transitioned from fringe speculation to a mainstream cultural phenomenon.

Project Blue Book: The Government's Secret Investigation

In response to the growing number of UFO sightings after World War II, the U.S. Air Force launched Project Blue Book in 1952. This was not the first government investigation into UFOs, but it was the most comprehensive, running until 1969. Over nearly two decades, Project Blue Book investigated over 12,000 reported UFO sightings, with the goal of determining whether they posed a threat to national security.

Most of the cases were ultimately explained as natural phenomena or misidentified aircraft, but a small percentage remained unexplained. These "unknowns" continue to fuel speculation that the government knows more about UFOs than it's willing to admit. The files from Project Blue Book were declassified in the 1970s, but the mystery only deepened as researchers pored over the documents, searching for clues.

One of the most compelling cases investigated by Project Blue Book was the 1952 Washington, D.C., UFO incident. Over several days in July, radar operators and pilots reported seeing strange lights and objects over the nation's capital. The sightings were witnessed by multiple credible sources, including military personnel, leading to widespread public concern. The Air Force eventually dismissed the sightings as temperature inversions, but not everyone was convinced.

The existence of Project Blue Book itself is a testament to how seriously the government took the UFO phenomenon, even as it publicly downplayed the significance of sightings. The project's legacy lives on in the ongoing debate over what, if anything, the government is hiding about UFOs.

Area 51: The Heart of the Conspiracy

If Roswell is the birthplace of UFO culture, then Area 51 is its beating heart. This top-secret military base in the Nevada desert has been the subject of speculation for decades, with rumours of alien spacecraft, underground labs, and reverse-engineered technology. Area 51 was officially acknowledged by the U.S. government only in 2013, but by then, it had already become a focal point for conspiracy theories.

The secrecy surrounding Area 51, combined with its remote location and high security, has made it the perfect breeding ground for speculation. Some former employees have come forward with stories of working on advanced aircraft that were mistaken for UFOs, but others claim to have seen much stranger things. The most famous of these is Bob Lazar, who in 1989 claimed to have worked on reverse-engineering alien technology at a site near Area 51. Lazar's story has been widely criticized, but it has also become a cornerstone of the UFO lore surrounding the base.

Area 51 represents the intersection of UFOs, government secrecy, and the public's thirst for answers. It's a place where the lines between fact and fiction blur, and where every piece of information—or disinformation—feeds into the larger narrative of a government cover-up.

Pop Culture and the UFO Phenomenon

The rise of UFO sightings in the 20th century coincided with the birth of modern pop culture, and the two have been intertwined ever since. From movies like *Close Encounters of the Third Kind* to TV shows like *The X-Files*, the idea of alien visitors has become a staple of entertainment. These portrayals have, in turn, influenced public perception of UFOs, creating a feedback loop where life imitates art and vice versa.

One of the earliest and most influential pieces of UFO-related pop culture was Orson Welles' 1938 radio broadcast of *The War of the Worlds*. Though not a real UFO event, the panic it allegedly caused demonstrated the public's fascination with the idea of an alien invasion. As UFO sightings became more common in the post-war years, Hollywood was quick to capitalize on the trend, with a wave of sci-fi films featuring flying saucers and alien invaders.

But it's not just fiction that has influenced the UFO phenomenon. In the 1990s, *The X-Files* captured the zeitgeist with its blend of government conspiracy, paranormal activity, and extraterrestrial intrigue. The show's catchphrase, "The truth is out there," became a rallying cry for UFO enthusiasts and conspiracy theorists alike. The influence of *The X-Files* can't be overstated—it not only shaped how people thought about UFOs but also inspired a new generation of investigators and believers.

Today, the influence of UFOs on pop culture is stronger than ever, with shows like *Ancient Aliens* and documentaries like *Unacknowledged* bringing the subject to mainstream audiences. But while pop culture has helped to keep the UFO phenomenon in the public eye, it has also made it harder to separate fact from fiction.

Government Disclosures and the Pentagon's UFO Report

In recent years, the debate over UFOs has taken a new turn with the release of previously classified government documents and footage. In 2017, The New York Times published an article revealing the existence of a secret Pentagon program called the Advanced Aerospace Threat Identification Program (AATIP), which investigated reports of UFOs from 2007 to 2012. The article included videos taken by Navy pilots showing unidentified objects performing manoeuvres that seemed to defy the laws of physics.

The release of these videos, along with the Pentagon's admission that UFOs are real and deserve serious study, marked a significant shift in the government's approach to the phenomenon. In June 2021, the Pentagon released a highly anticipated report on UFOs, or Unidentified Aerial Phenomena (UAPs) as they are now called. The report examined 144 cases of UAP encounters by military personnel, of which only one could be definitively explained. The rest remain a mystery.

While the report stopped short of confirming the existence of extraterrestrial life, it acknowledged that these objects are real, and that they pose a potential threat to national security. For many, this was a long-awaited validation of what they've believed for years: that the government knows more about UFOs than it's been willing to admit.

But the report also raised new questions. If these objects aren't extraterrestrial, then what are they? Advanced technology from a foreign adversary? Or something else entirely? The Pentagon's report may have provided more questions than answers, but it has certainly reignited public interest in the UFO phenomenon.

Conclusion: The Ongoing Mystery

As we've seen in this chapter, the modern UFO phenomenon is a complex and multifaceted issue, involving government secrecy, public fascination, and a healthy dose of scepticism. Whether you believe that UFOs are evidence of extraterrestrial visitors or simply misidentified natural phenomena, there's no denying the impact they've had on our culture and our collective imagination.

In the next chapter, we'll explore the more personal side of the UFO phenomenon: the stories of those who claim to have had close encounters with alien beings. These accounts, often dismissed by sceptics, offer a glimpse into the lives of people who have experienced something truly unexplainable. As we continue our journey, keep in mind that the truth might be stranger than we ever imagined

CHAPTER 3:
ABDUCTIONS AND
CLOSE ENCOUNTERS

While UFO sightings have captivated the public for decades, the stories of alien abductions and close encounters add a deeply personal and often unsettling dimension to the phenomenon. Unlike the fleeting glimpse of a strange light in the sky, abductions and close encounters involve intimate, often terrifying experiences that leave lasting psychological and physical effects on those who claim to have been taken. In this chapter, we'll explore some of the most famous and credible abduction cases, examine the common elements that appear in these stories, and consider the implications for those who have lived through these harrowing events.

The Betty and Barney Hill Abduction: The First Widely Reported Case

Our exploration begins with what is often regarded as the first widely reported alien abduction case: the experience of Betty and Barney Hill. The Hills were an ordinary couple living in New Hampshire, but their lives changed forever on the night of September 19, 1961. As they were driving home from a vacation in Canada, they noticed a strange light in the sky that seemed to be following them. What happened next is a story that has become iconic in UFO lore.

According to the Hills, the light eventually revealed itself to be a large, disc-shaped craft that hovered over their car. They heard a buzzing noise, and then their memories became fragmented. When they "awoke," they found themselves 35 miles further along their route, with no recollection of how they got there. Over the following weeks, both Betty and Barney began experiencing strange dreams and flashbacks, leading them to seek the help of a psychiatrist who specialized in hypnosis.

Under hypnosis, the Hills recounted a detailed story of being taken aboard the UFO by humanoid beings with large eyes and grey skin—an image that has since become the archetype of the "grey" alien. The beings allegedly performed medical examinations on the couple and communicated with them telepathically. Betty even claimed to have been shown a star map, which she later recreated under hypnosis.

The Hill abduction case became the subject of intense media scrutiny and has been studied by numerous researchers over the years. While sceptics argue that the story could be a product of stress, sleep deprivation, or cultural influences, the Hills' account remains one of the most well-documented and influential abduction stories. It set the template for many of the abduction reports that would follow, including themes of missing time, medical procedures, and telepathic communication.

The Travis Walton Abduction: A Case That Divides Opinion

Another high-profile abduction case occurred on November 5, 1975, when a young logger named Travis Walton disappeared for five days in the forests of Arizona. Walton's experience, later dramatized in the movie *Fire in the Sky*, is one of the most controversial and debated abduction cases in history.

Walton and his co-workers were driving home after a day of logging when they saw a bright light in the sky. Walton, curious, got out of the truck to get a closer look. According to his co-workers, a beam of light struck Walton, lifting him off the ground and throwing him several feet away. Terrified, the others drove off, only to return minutes later to find Walton gone.

Walton reappeared five days later, disoriented and with no memory of where he had been. Under hypnosis, he later described being taken aboard a spacecraft and encountering both humanoid and non-human entities. His story included elements common to other abduction reports: medical examinations, telepathic communication, and a sense of profound fear.

The Walton case has been the subject of numerous investigations, including polygraph tests, which Walton and his co-workers passed, adding credibility to their story. However, sceptics argue that the incident could have been a hoax or the result of a psychological breakdown. Despite the controversy, Walton's account remains one of the most compelling and well-documented abduction cases, and it continues to inspire both believers and sceptics alike.

Patterns in Abduction Narratives: Common Themes and Experiences

As more and more people have come forward with their own abduction stories, researchers have identified several common themes and patterns that appear in these narratives. While each case is unique, certain elements seem to recur, suggesting that these experiences might be part of a larger phenomenon.

- **Medical Examinations**: Many abductees report undergoing invasive medical procedures, often involving needles, implants, or other instruments. These examinations are typically performed by small, gray-skinned beings with large eyes, who work methodically and without apparent emotion. Abductees often describe feeling paralyzed or unable to resist during these procedures.

- **Missing Time**: A recurring feature of abduction stories is the experience of "missing time." Abductees often describe being taken while performing everyday activities, only to "wake up" hours or even days later with no memory of what happened in between. This missing time is often accompanied by feelings of confusion, disorientation, and anxiety.

- **Telepathic Communication**: Many abductees report that the beings they encounter communicate with them telepathically, conveying thoughts, images, or emotions directly into their minds. This form of communication is often described as clear and direct, yet difficult to fully comprehend or articulate afterward.

- **Implants and Physical Evidence**: Some abductees claim to have discovered small, unexplained implants in their bodies following their experiences. These implants are often described as metallic or crystalline objects, and in some cases, they have been surgically removed and analysed. While sceptics argue that these could be mundane objects or the result of self-inflicted injuries, others see them as evidence of alien technology.

- **Psychological and Emotional Impact**: Abduction experiences often leave a lasting impact on those who claim to have gone through them. Many report symptoms similar to post-traumatic stress disorder (PTSD), including nightmares, flashbacks, anxiety, and depression. Some also describe a profound shift in their worldview, feeling disconnected from everyday life or convinced that they have a special purpose related to their experience.

Scepticism and Alternative Explanations

While the accounts of abductions and close encounters are compelling, they are also met with considerable scepticism..

Many researchers argue that these experiences could be explained by psychological factors, such as sleep paralysis, false memories, or cultural influences. Sleep paralysis, for example, is a well-documented phenomenon in which a person experiences a temporary inability to move or speak while falling asleep or waking up, often accompanied by vivid hallucinations. Some suggest that abduction experiences might be a modern manifestation of this condition.

Others point to the influence of media and popular culture in shaping these narratives. The image of the "grey" alien, for example, has become so ubiquitous that it may influence how people interpret strange or unexplained experiences. Additionally, the use of hypnosis in recovering abduction memories is controversial, as it can sometimes lead to the creation of false memories.

However, for many abductees, these alternative explanations fail to capture the reality of their experiences. They argue that their memories are too vivid, too detailed, and too consistent with those of other abductees to be easily dismissed. For these individuals, the scepticism of others only adds to the trauma of their experiences, leaving them isolated and unsure of whom to trust.

The Role of Support Groups and Abduction Researchers

For those who have experienced abductions, finding a community of support can be crucial in coping with the psychological and emotional aftermath. Over the years, numerous support groups have formed, providing a safe space for abductees to share their stories and find validation among others who have had similar experiences.

Organizations like the Mutual UFO Network (MUFON) and the Center for UFO Studies (CUFOS) have also played a key role in documenting abduction cases and providing resources for those affected. Researchers like Budd Hopkins, John Mack, and David Jacobs have conducted extensive studies on abduction experiences, often using hypnosis to help abductees recover lost memories and come to terms with their experiences.

These researchers have contributed significantly to our understanding of the abduction phenomenon, though their work is not without controversy. Some in the scientific community criticize the use of hypnosis and question the reliability of recovered memories. Despite this, the work of abduction researchers has provided a framework for understanding these experiences and has helped many abductees find meaning in what they've gone through.

Conclusion: The Mystery of Close Encounters

The stories of alien abductions and close encounters are among the most compelling and disturbing aspects of the UFO phenomenon. Whether you believe these accounts represent real encounters with extraterrestrial beings or are the result of psychological or cultural influences, there's no denying the profound impact they have on those who experience them. These stories challenge our understanding of reality and push the boundaries of what we consider possible.

In the next chapter, we'll expand our exploration beyond individual experiences to look at how different cultures around the world interpret and experience alien encounters. From South America to Africa, UFO sightings and close encounters are a global phenomenon, shaped by cultural beliefs and traditions. As we continue our journey, we'll see how the mystery of alien contact transcends borders and connects us all in our search for answers

CHAPTER 4: GLOBAL SIGHTINGS AND CULTURAL INTERPRETATIONS

The phenomenon of UFO sightings and alien encounters is not confined to any one country or culture. From the remote jungles of South America to the deserts of Africa, reports of strange lights in the sky and mysterious beings have been recorded across the globe. In this chapter, we'll explore how different cultures interpret these experiences, and how their unique worldviews and traditions shape their understanding of what these encounters might mean. This exploration will show us that while the specifics of these stories may vary, the underlying mystery— and the human response to it—is universal.

UFO Sightings in South America: The Chupas of Brazil

Let's begin our journey in South America, a region with a rich history of UFO sightings and encounters. One of the most intriguing cases comes from Brazil, where reports of "chupas"— small, metallic UFOs that emit beams of light—have been a persistent part of local lore.

The term "chupa" is derived from the Portuguese word for "sucker," referring to the belief that these objects drain energy from living things. In the late 1970s and early 1980s, the region of Maranhão in northern Brazil became the epicentre of a series of chupa sightings. Villagers reported seeing small, glowing objects that would hover above the treetops or near the ground, emitting beams of intense light. Those caught in the light beam often experienced symptoms such as burns, nausea, and weakness, leading many to fear these mysterious visitors.

The Brazilian government took these reports seriously, launching an investigation known as Operation Saucer (Operação Prato). The operation, led by the Brazilian Air Force, involved extensive fieldwork, including interviews with witnesses and attempts to capture photographic evidence of the chupas. While the official results of the investigation were inconclusive, the operation added a layer of credibility to the villagers' reports and fuelled further speculation about the nature of these mysterious objects.

The chupa phenomenon highlights how cultural context can influence the interpretation of UFO encounters. In Brazil, where traditional beliefs in spirits and supernatural beings are still strong in rural areas, the chupas are often seen as malevolent entities rather than visitors from another planet. This interpretation is shaped by local folklore, which includes numerous stories of spirits and creatures that prey on the living.

The Foo Fighters: UFOs in the Skies of World War II

During World War II, both Allied and Axis pilots reported seeing strange, glowing objects following their planes during combat missions. These objects, which became known as "foo fighters," were described as balls of light that moved at incredible speeds, often performing manoeuvres that seemed impossible for any known aircraft of the time.

The foo fighters were most commonly reported in the skies over Europe and the Pacific, and their presence was a source of great concern for military personnel. Initially, both sides suspected that these objects were some kind of advanced enemy technology, perhaps a new type of weapon or surveillance device. However, as reports continued to come in from both Allied and Axis pilots, it became clear that neither side was responsible for these mysterious objects.

Despite numerous sightings and even some attempts to engage the foo fighters, no definitive explanation was ever found. Some pilots described the objects as playful or curious, following their planes closely but never engaging in hostile actions. Others, however, reported feeling a sense of unease or even terror when encountering these lights.

The term "foo fighter" itself is derived from the comic strip *Smokey Stover*, in which the character Smokey frequently used the nonsensical phrase, "Where there's foo, there's fire!" The term was adopted by American pilots to describe these mysterious lights, and it has since become a part of UFO lore.

The foo fighter phenomenon is a fascinating example of how different cultures and circumstances can lead to different interpretations of the same phenomenon. During the war, these objects were seen through the lens of military strategy and technological competition. Today, they are often discussed in the context of UFO sightings and potential extraterrestrial contact.

The Rendlesham Forest Incident: The UK's Roswell

One of the most famous UFO incidents in the United Kingdom occurred in late December 1980, near the Rendlesham Forest in Suffolk. Often referred to as "Britain's Roswell," the Rendlesham Forest incident involved multiple witnesses, including military personnel from the nearby RAF Bentwaters and RAF Woodbridge airbases.

The incident began in the early hours of December 26, when security personnel at the base reported seeing strange lights in the forest. A small team was sent to investigate, and what they found has since become the stuff of legend. According to their reports, they encountered a triangular craft with strange markings on its surface. The craft emitted a bright light and appeared to hover above the ground. When the men attempted to approach it, the craft moved away and eventually disappeared into the night.

Over the next two nights, more sightings were reported, and one of the witnesses, Lieutenant Colonel Charles Halt, even recorded his observations on a tape recorder as he and his team investigated the area. The recordings, which capture Halt's descriptions of the lights and his growing sense of disbelief, have become key pieces of evidence in the case.

The Rendlesham Forest incident has been the subject of numerous investigations and documentaries, and it remains one of the most credible and well-documented UFO cases in history. However, like many UFO incidents, it is also surrounded by controversy. Some sceptics have suggested that the lights seen by the witnesses were merely misidentified aircraft or natural phenomena, while others believe that the entire incident was a case of mass hysteria.

Despite these explanations, the Rendlesham Forest incident continues to be a major point of interest for UFO researchers and enthusiasts. It's a case that highlights how UFO sightings can captivate the public imagination and become part of a nation's cultural heritage.

UFOs and Spirituality in Africa: The Zimbabwe School Encounter

In many parts of Africa, UFO sightings and encounters are often interpreted through the lens of spirituality and traditional beliefs. One of the most intriguing cases occurred in Zimbabwe in 1994, when a group of schoolchildren at the Ariel School in Ruwa reported seeing a strange craft and beings near their playground.

On the morning of September 16, 1994, 62 children between the ages of six and twelve witnessed a silver, disc-shaped object land in a field near their school. The children described seeing small beings with large eyes emerge from the craft. The beings reportedly communicated with the children telepathically, conveying messages about the dangers of environmental destruction and the importance of caring for the planet.

What makes this case particularly compelling is the consistency of the children's accounts, despite being interviewed separately and having no previous exposure to UFO stories. The case was investigated by a number of researchers, including the Harvard psychiatrist John Mack, who found the children's testimonies to be credible and deeply moving.

In Zimbabwe, where traditional beliefs in spirits and ancestors are still prevalent, the children's encounter was often interpreted as a visit from spiritual beings rather than extraterrestrial visitors. This interpretation reflects the way in which cultural and spiritual beliefs can shape the understanding of unexplained phenomena.

The Zimbabwe school encounter is a powerful example of how UFO experiences can transcend cultural boundaries and raise questions that resonate with people from all walks of life. Whether seen as a spiritual message or a visit from another world, the incident left a lasting impact on those who experienced it and continues to be a subject of fascination for researchers.

Conclusion: A Global Phenomenon

As we've seen in this chapter, UFO sightings and encounters are a global phenomenon, experienced by people from all cultures and backgrounds. While the specifics of these encounters may vary, the underlying themes—mystery, fear, wonder, and a search for meaning—are universal.

Different cultures interpret these experiences through their own lenses, whether it's the spiritual traditions of Africa, the military context of World War II, or the folklore of rural Brazil. These interpretations add richness and depth to the global tapestry of UFO encounters, reminding us that the question of whether we are alone in the universe is one that resonates with people everywhere.

In the next chapter, we'll turn our attention to the scientific side of the phenomenon, exploring the search for extraterrestrial life and the scientific explanations for UFO sightings. As we delve into the science behind the mystery, we'll see how our understanding of the universe is constantly evolving and how the search for answers continues to push the boundaries of human knowledge

CHAPTER 5: THE SCIENCE BEHIND THE PHENOMENON

While stories of UFO sightings and alien encounters have captivated the public imagination, the scientific community has approached the question of extraterrestrial life with a combination of curiosity, scepticism, and rigor. In this chapter, we'll explore the scientific efforts to investigate UFOs and the broader search for life beyond Earth. We'll look at the ongoing quest to find habitable planets, the challenges of detecting extraterrestrial civilizations, and the scientific theories that might explain some of the strange phenomena reported around the world.

The Search for Exoplanets: Finding Other Earths

One of the most exciting developments in modern astronomy has been the discovery of exoplanets—planets that orbit stars outside our solar system. For decades, scientists speculated that other stars might have planets, but it wasn't until the 1990s that the first exoplanets were confirmed. Since then, the search for exoplanets has accelerated, with thousands of these distant worlds now catalogued.

The discovery of exoplanets has profound implications for the search for extraterrestrial life. If Earth is not unique in having the conditions necessary for life, then it's possible that other planets might also harbour living organisms. The search for exoplanets has focused on identifying those in the "habitable zone," the region around a star where conditions might be right for liquid water—a key ingredient for life as we know it.

The Kepler Space Telescope, launched in 2009, revolutionized the search for exoplanets by using the transit method to detect planets passing in front of their stars. Kepler's discoveries have included a wide variety of exoplanets, some similar in size and composition to Earth. The most promising of these are referred to as "Earth-like" or "super-Earths," and they represent our best chance of finding a planet where life might exist.

However, finding an exoplanet in the habitable zone is just the first step. The next challenge is determining whether these planets have atmospheres and, if so, what those atmospheres are made of. Scientists are developing new techniques to analyse the light from distant planets, looking for chemical signatures that might indicate the presence of life. This is a complex and challenging task, but it's one that could provide definitive evidence of extraterrestrial life.

The discovery of even a single exoplanet with signs of life would be a groundbreaking moment in human history. It would confirm that we are not alone in the universe and would raise profound questions about the nature of life and our place in the cosmos.

The Drake Equation: Estimating the Number of Civilizations

In 1961, the astronomer Frank Drake proposed an equation to estimate the number of extraterrestrial civilizations in our galaxy with which we might be able to communicate. The Drake Equation has become a central tool in the search for extraterrestrial intelligence (SETI), providing a framework for thinking about the factors that might influence the development of life and civilizations elsewhere in the galaxy.

The Drake Equation is expressed as:

$$N = R_* \times f_p \times n_e \times f_l \times f_i \times f_c \times L$$

Where:

- **N** is the number of civilizations with which humans could communicate.

- **R*** is the average rate of star formation in our galaxy.

- **f_p** is the fraction of those stars that have planetary systems.

- **n_e** is the average number of planets that could potentially support life per star with planets.

- **f_l** is the fraction of those planets where life actually develops.

- **f_i** is the fraction of planets with life where intelligent life evolves.

- **f_c** is the fraction of civilizations that develop technology detectable by us.

- **L** is the length of time such civilizations release detectable signals into space.

Each of these factors is uncertain, leading to a wide range of possible values for N. If we are optimistic about the likelihood of each factor, the equation suggests there could be many civilizations in the galaxy. However, if we take a more conservative view, the number of civilizations might be very small—or even zero.

The Drake Equation is more than just a mathematical formula; it's a way of thinking about the challenges and opportunities in the search for extraterrestrial life. It highlights the many steps required for a civilization to develop to the point where it can communicate across the stars, and it underscores the importance of continued exploration and discovery.

The Fermi Paradox: If Aliens Exist, Where Are They?

The idea that intelligent extraterrestrial civilizations might exist leads us to one of the most puzzling questions in science: the Fermi Paradox. Named after the physicist Enrico Fermi, who famously asked, "Where is everybody?" during a discussion about the possibility of alien life, the paradox highlights the apparent contradiction between the high probability of extraterrestrial civilizations and the lack of evidence for or contact with them.

There are several possible explanations for the Fermi Paradox, each with profound implications:

- **Rare Earth Hypothesis**: One explanation is that Earth-like planets are extremely rare, and the conditions that allowed life to develop on Earth are so unique that they haven't been replicated elsewhere in the galaxy. This idea suggests that while microbial life might be common, intelligent life is exceedingly rare.

- **Great Filter**: Another possibility is that there is a "Great Filter" somewhere in the process of developing intelligent life, a step that is extremely difficult or unlikely. This filter could be in our past, meaning that we've already overcome the hardest part of evolution, or it could be in our future, meaning that most civilizations self-destruct before reaching the point where they can communicate with others.

- **Advanced Civilizations Are Hiding**: Some theories suggest that advanced civilizations might be deliberately avoiding contact with us, either because they follow a "prime directive" of non-interference or because they see no benefit in communicating with a less advanced species.

- **We're Not Looking in the Right Way**: It's also possible that we simply haven't been searching for extraterrestrial civilizations in the right way. Our methods of detecting signals might be too primitive, or we might be looking for the wrong kinds of evidence. Advanced civilizations might communicate in ways that we can't yet detect or understand.

The Fermi Paradox remains one of the most intriguing questions in the search for extraterrestrial life. It challenges us to think about the nature of life, intelligence, and civilization in a broader cosmic context.

SETI: The Search for Extraterrestrial Intelligence

One of the most direct ways to search for extraterrestrial life is through the efforts of SETI, the Search for Extraterrestrial Intelligence. SETI involves scanning the skies for signals—usually in the form of radio waves—that might indicate the presence of a technologically advanced civilization.

The idea behind SETI is simple: if an advanced civilization exists and is trying to communicate, it might be sending out signals that we could detect. By using powerful radio telescopes, scientists can listen for these signals and analyse them for patterns that might indicate they're of intelligent origin.

One of the most famous moments in SETI's history came in 1977, when astronomer Jerry R. Ehman detected a strong, narrowband radio signal from the constellation Sagittarius. This signal, known as the "Wow! signal," lasted for 72 seconds and has never been detected again. Despite extensive analysis, the Wow! signal remains unexplained and is one of the best candidates for a potential extraterrestrial transmission.

SETI has faced many challenges over the years, including limited funding and the sheer vastness of space to search. However, advances in technology, including the use of artificial intelligence to analyse data, have renewed interest in the project. While SETI has yet to find definitive proof of extraterrestrial life, the search continues, driven by the belief that if intelligent civilizations exist, we might one day hear from them.

The Science of UFOs: Rational Explanations for Unexplained Phenomena

While the search for extraterrestrial life often focuses on finding distant civilizations, the study of UFOs involves investigating strange phenomena closer to home. Many UFO sightings can be explained by natural or man-made causes, but some remain mysterious and continue to puzzle scientists.

One of the main challenges in studying UFOs is the lack of consistent, reliable data. Most sightings are anecdotal and involve only brief glimpses of strange objects or lights. However, in some cases, more substantial evidence, such as radar data or physical traces, has been collected.

Several scientific explanations have been proposed for UFO sightings:

- **Natural Phenomena**: Some UFO sightings can be attributed to natural phenomena such as meteorites, ball lightning, or atmospheric reflections. These events can produce strange lights or objects that might be mistaken for alien spacecraft.

- **Man-Made Objects**: Many UFO sightings turn out to be misidentified aircraft, satellites, weather balloons, or even space debris. In some cases, experimental military aircraft have been mistaken for UFOs, particularly during the Cold War when secrecy about advanced technology was paramount.

- **Psychological Factors**: Human perception is not always reliable, and psychological factors can play a significant role in UFO sightings. Optical illusions, fatigue, and the power of suggestion can all influence what people believe they see. In some cases, mass hysteria has led to multiple people reporting the same UFO sighting, even when there was no actual object present.

While many UFO sightings can be explained by these factors, some cases defy easy explanation. These "unidentified" cases are often the focus of intense investigation and debate, with some scientists advocating for more rigorous study of the phenomenon.

Conclusion: The Ongoing Quest for Answers

The scientific search for extraterrestrial life and the investigation of UFOs represent two sides of the same coin. Both are driven by a fundamental curiosity about our place in the universe and a desire to understand the unknown. While science has made great strides in recent decades—discovering exoplanets, refining our estimates of the likelihood of extraterrestrial civilizations, and developing new tools for detecting alien signals—many questions remain unanswered.

The mystery of UFOs continues to challenge our understanding of the world around us, while the search for extraterrestrial life pushes the boundaries of our knowledge and technology. Whether or not we ever find definitive proof of alien life, these efforts remind us of the vastness of the cosmos and the many mysteries it still holds.

In the next chapter, we'll explore the role of government disclosures and the testimonies of whistleblowers in the ongoing debate about UFOs and extraterrestrial contact. As we delve into the secretive world of military investigations and classified documents, we'll see how the quest for truth has often been complicated by secrecy and misinformation.

CHAPTER 6: GOVERNMENT DISCLOSURES AND WHISTLEBLOWERS

The relationship between governments and the UFO phenomenon has always been shrouded in secrecy and suspicion. Over the decades, various governments, particularly that of the United States, have been accused of covering up evidence of extraterrestrial encounters, leading to widespread speculation and conspiracy theories. In recent years, however, there has been a shift toward greater transparency, with governments releasing previously classified information and whistleblowers coming forward with startling claims. In this chapter, we'll explore the history of government involvement in UFO investigations, the significance of recent disclosures, and the testimonies of individuals who claim to have firsthand knowledge of extraterrestrial encounters.

The History of Government Involvement: From Project Blue Book to the Pentagon's UFO Programs

Government interest in UFOs began in earnest after World War II, as sightings of strange objects in the sky became more common. In response to public concern, the U.S. Air Force launched a series of investigations into UFO reports, the most famous of which was Project Blue Book. Running from 1952 to 1969, Project Blue

Book was tasked with determining whether UFOs posed a threat to national security and whether they could be scientifically explained.

During its operation, Project Blue Book investigated over 12,000 UFO reports. The majority of these were explained as misidentified aircraft, weather phenomena, or other natural occurrences. However, a small percentage—roughly 701 cases—remained unexplained, fuelling speculation that the government was hiding something.

The official conclusion of Project Blue Book was that UFOs did not pose a threat to national security and that there was no evidence to suggest they were of extraterrestrial origin. However, many researchers and UFO enthusiasts believe that this conclusion was designed to calm public fears rather than reflect the true nature of the phenomenon.

In the decades following the closure of Project Blue Book, the U.S. government continued to monitor UFO activity, though often in secret. One of the most significant revelations came in 2017 when The New York Times published an article revealing the existence of the Advanced Aerospace Threat Identification Program (AATIP), a secret Pentagon program that investigated UFO reports from 2007 to 2012.

AATIP was initially funded at the request of then-Senate Majority Leader Harry Reid and focused on reports of UFO encounters by military personnel. The program collected and analysed data, including video footage captured by Navy pilots, some of which showed unidentified objects performing manoeuvres that seemed to defy the laws of physics.

The release of AATIP's existence, along with the accompanying videos, marked a turning point in the government's approach to UFOs. For the first time in decades, the U.S. government acknowledged that UFOs—now referred to as Unidentified Aerial Phenomena (UAPs)—were real and deserved serious study.

The Pentagon's UFO Report: A New Era of Transparency?

In June 2021, the Pentagon released a long-awaited report on UAPs, responding to a request from Congress for greater transparency on the issue. The report, which examined 144 UAP encounters reported by military personnel between 2004 and 2021, was a major milestone in the government's handling of UFOs.

The report's findings were both revealing and frustratingly vague. Of the 144 cases studied, only one could be definitively explained—a sighting that turned out to be a large, deflating balloon. The remaining 143 cases included sightings of objects that exhibited unusual flight characteristics, such as sudden acceleration, the ability to move at high speeds without visible propulsion, and the capability to manoeuvre in ways that would be impossible for known aircraft.

While the report stopped short of concluding that these objects were of extraterrestrial origin, it did acknowledge that they posed a potential threat to national security and warranted further investigation. The report also highlighted the need for improved data collection and analysis, suggesting that future studies might yield more conclusive results.

The release of the Pentagon's UAP report was a significant step toward greater government transparency on the issue of UFOs. However, it also raised new questions about what the government knows and what it is still keeping secret. For many UFO researchers and enthusiasts, the report was a long-overdue acknowledgment of what they had suspected for years: that something strange is happening in our skies, and that the government is taking it seriously.

Whistleblowers and Insiders: Testimonies from Those in the Know

While official government disclosures have provided some insight into the UFO phenomenon, some of the most intriguing and controversial information has come from whistleblowers—individuals who claim to have firsthand knowledge of secret government programs related to extraterrestrial encounters.

One of the most famous whistleblowers in the UFO community is Bob Lazar, who in 1989 claimed that he had worked at a site near Area 51 on reverse-engineering alien technology. According to Lazar, he was tasked with studying a spacecraft of extraterrestrial origin, attempting to understand how it operated and what technologies it used. Lazar's claims have been met with scepticism by many, and he has faced significant scrutiny regarding his background and credentials. However, his story has also attracted a large following and remains a cornerstone of modern UFO lore.

Another notable whistleblower is Dr. Steven Greer, a former emergency room physician who founded the Disclosure Project, an organization dedicated to revealing the truth about UFOs and extraterrestrial life. Greer has compiled testimonies from hundreds of former military personnel, government officials, and contractors who claim to have knowledge of UFO encounters, government cover-ups, and even secret programs involving extraterrestrial beings. While Greer's claims are often dismissed by sceptics, his work has brought considerable attention to the issue of government secrecy and has inspired a movement of individuals seeking full disclosure.

More recently, former military and intelligence officials have also come forward with their own experiences. Luis Elizondo, a former Pentagon official who led the AATIP program, has become one of the most vocal advocates for greater transparency on the issue of UAPs. Elizondo has spoken publicly about the need for a serious, scientific investigation into these phenomena and has suggested that the government knows more than it has revealed.

These whistleblowers and insiders offer tantalizing glimpses into a world of secrecy and intrigue, where advanced technology, extraterrestrial encounters, and government cover-ups may be intertwined. Their testimonies are often controversial and difficult to verify, but they have played a crucial role in keeping the UFO debate alive and pushing for greater transparency.

The Debate Over Government Transparency and Public Knowledge

The question of how much the government knows about UFOs and extraterrestrial life—and how much it is willing to reveal —remains a contentious issue. For decades, conspiracy theorists have accused the government of withholding information from the public, citing incidents like Roswell and Area 51 as evidence of a cover-up. While some of these claims may be exaggerated, the government's own actions have often fuelled these suspicions.

The decision to keep certain information classified, such as the details of military encounters with UAPs, is often justified on the grounds of national security. The concern is that revealing too much could expose sensitive technologies or strategies to potential adversaries. However, this secrecy also creates an environment where speculation and mistrust can thrive.

In recent years, the push for greater transparency has gained momentum, driven by a combination of public interest, media attention, and political pressure. The release of the Pentagon's UAP report and the declassification of AATIP documents are signs that the government is becoming more open about its investigations into UFOs. However, many believe that this is just the tip of the iceberg and that much more information remains hidden.

The debate over government transparency is not just about UFOs; it's also about the public's right to know. In a democratic society, the argument goes, citizens have a right to be informed about matters that could have profound implications for humanity. Whether or not the government is hiding the truth about extraterrestrial life, the demand for greater openness is unlikely to go away anytime soon.

Conclusion: The Quest for the Truth

The relationship between governments and the UFO phenomenon is complex and often contradictory. While official investigations like Project Blue Book and AATIP have sought to understand the nature of UFOs, the secrecy surrounding these programs has led to widespread suspicion and speculation. Recent disclosures and the testimonies of whistleblowers have brought new information to light, but they have also raised new questions.

As we've seen in this chapter, the quest for the truth about UFOs and extraterrestrial encounters is far from over. The government's role in this quest is both critical and controversial, and the balance between transparency and secrecy will continue to be a key issue in the years to come.

In the final chapter, we'll explore the broader implications of the UFO phenomenon for human society. We'll consider how these encounters challenge our understanding of reality, what they mean for our place in the universe, and how we might prepare for a future in which contact with extraterrestrial beings is confirmed

CHAPTER 7: THE IMPACT OF ALIEN ENCOUNTERS ON HUMAN SOCIETY

The possibility of contact with extraterrestrial beings is more than just a question of scientific curiosity; it is a profound issue that touches on the very essence of what it means to be human. Alien encounters, whether real or imagined, challenge our understanding of reality, our place in the universe, and our future as a species. In this final chapter, we'll explore the psychological, social, and philosophical implications of UFOs and potential extraterrestrial contact. We'll consider how these encounters might reshape our worldview, influence our societies, and change the course of human history.

The Psychological Effects of Alien Encounters

For those who claim to have experienced alien encounters, the psychological impact can be profound and long-lasting. Whether it's a brief sighting of a strange object in the sky or a full-fledged abduction experience, these encounters often leave individuals grappling with feelings of fear, confusion, and isolation. The sense of having experienced something extraordinary, yet being unable to fully explain or share it, can be deeply unsettling.

Many abductees report symptoms similar to post-traumatic stress disorder (PTSD), including nightmares, flashbacks, anxiety, and a heightened sense of vulnerability. These individuals often struggle to integrate their experiences into their everyday lives, leading to feelings of alienation from friends, family, and society. The fear of ridicule or disbelief can exacerbate this isolation, making it difficult for them to seek support or understanding.

In response to these challenges, support groups and communities have formed to provide a safe space for those who have had alien encounters. These groups offer validation, shared experiences, and a sense of belonging, helping individuals to cope with the psychological aftermath of their experiences. However, the stigma surrounding UFOs and alien abductions remains a significant barrier, and many continue to suffer in silence.

The psychological impact of alien encounters is not limited to those who have had direct experiences. The broader public, too, is affected by the possibility of extraterrestrial life. The idea that we might not be alone in the universe can be both thrilling and terrifying, sparking a range of emotions from excitement to existential dread. For some, the thought of alien contact is a source of hope, offering the possibility of new knowledge and a broader understanding of the cosmos. For others, it is a source of fear, raising concerns about the unknown and the potential threats that might come with it.

The Social and Cultural Impact: Shifting Paradigms

The social and cultural implications of alien encounters are far-reaching. Throughout history, humanity's understanding of its place in the universe has been shaped by religion, philosophy, and science. The confirmation of extraterrestrial life—or even widespread belief in its existence—could challenge these foundational beliefs and lead to a profound shift in our collective worldview.

One of the most significant areas of impact would likely be religion. Most of the world's major religions are based on the idea that humanity holds a special place in the cosmos, often with a unique relationship to the divine. The discovery of intelligent extraterrestrial beings could challenge these beliefs, raising questions about the nature of the soul, the uniqueness of human life, and the role of God in a universe populated by multiple intelligent species.

Religious scholars and leaders have already begun to grapple with these questions, exploring how traditional beliefs might be reconciled with the existence of extraterrestrial life. Some see the potential for a broader, more inclusive understanding of the divine, while others warn of the potential for conflict and confusion. The impact on religion would vary widely depending on the nature of the contact and the specific beliefs of different cultures and communities.

The confirmation of extraterrestrial life would also have profound implications for science and philosophy. Our understanding of life, consciousness, and the evolution of intelligence would be challenged and expanded. The discovery of alien life could lead to new fields of study, new technologies, and a deeper understanding of the cosmos and our place within it.

Culturally, the impact of alien encounters would be felt in a variety of ways. Literature, film, and other forms of art have long explored the idea of extraterrestrial contact, often reflecting our hopes, fears, and uncertainties about the unknown. The confirmation of alien life would inspire a new wave of creative expression, as artists and writers seek to grapple with the implications of this new reality.

At the same time, the social and political structures of human societies would be tested by the challenges and opportunities posed by extraterrestrial contact. Issues of governance, diplomacy, and ethics would come to the fore as humanity navigates its relationship with other intelligent beings. Questions about sovereignty, rights, and the protection of Earth's environment and resources would take on new urgency in the context of a larger, inhabited universe.

The Philosophical Implications: What Does It Mean to Be Human?

The discovery of extraterrestrial life would force us to confront some of the most profound philosophical questions about our existence. What does it mean to be human in a universe where we are not alone? How do we define intelligence, consciousness, and personhood in a broader cosmic context? What are the moral and ethical obligations of humans toward other intelligent beings, and how do we navigate the complexities of interspecies communication and interaction?

One of the central questions is the issue of human exceptionalism —the idea that humanity is unique and special in the universe. This belief has shaped much of our history, from our religious traditions to our scientific endeavours. The confirmation of extraterrestrial life would challenge this notion, forcing us to reconsider our place in the cosmos and our relationship to other forms of life.

The question of intelligence is also central to this philosophical inquiry. How do we define intelligence, and how do we recognize it in beings that might be vastly different from ourselves? The discovery of intelligent extraterrestrial life could lead to a redefinition of intelligence, consciousness, and even life itself. It could also challenge our understanding of ethics and morality, as we consider the rights and responsibilities of interacting with other intelligent species.

Another important philosophical question is the issue of communication. How do we communicate with beings that might have different senses, languages, and modes of thought? The challenges of interspecies communication would raise new questions about the nature of language, meaning, and understanding. It would also force us to confront the limitations of our own knowledge and the potential for misunderstanding and conflict.

Ultimately, the discovery of extraterrestrial life would force us to confront our own humanity in a new and profound way. It would challenge us to think beyond the boundaries of our own species, our own planet, and our own history, and to consider our place in a much larger, more complex, and more mysterious universe.

Preparing for the Future: The Possibility of Contact

As we consider the impact of alien encounters on human society, it's important to think about how we might prepare for the possibility of contact. While the discovery of extraterrestrial life is still hypothetical, the implications are so significant that it warrants serious consideration.

One area of preparation involves the development of protocols and guidelines for how to respond to contact. Governments, scientists, and international organizations have begun to explore these issues, considering questions such as: How should we communicate with extraterrestrial beings? What should be the role of national governments versus international bodies in managing contact? How should we handle the potential risks and opportunities of contact, including the possibility of cultural exchange, technological transfer, and the protection of Earth's environment and resources?

Another important area of preparation is public education and engagement. The discovery of extraterrestrial life would be a momentous event, and it's important that the public is informed and prepared for the implications. This includes not only understanding the scientific and technological aspects of contact but also considering the social, cultural, and philosophical questions that it raises.

Finally, we must consider the ethical implications of contact. How do we ensure that our interactions with extraterrestrial beings are conducted in a way that respects their rights and dignity, as well as the rights and dignity of all life on Earth? This includes thinking about issues such as the potential for exploitation, the risks of cultural imperialism, and the importance of protecting the environment and resources of both Earth and other planets.

Conclusion: A New Era for Humanity

The possibility of contact with extraterrestrial beings is one of the most profound questions facing humanity. It challenges our understanding of who we are, where we come from, and where we are going. While the discovery of alien life is still uncertain, the impact of this possibility is already being felt in our culture, our science, and our philosophy.

As we move into the future, it's important that we approach the question of extraterrestrial life with an open mind, a sense of curiosity, and a commitment to ethical and responsible behaviour. Whether or not we ever make contact with other intelligent beings, the search for answers will continue to shape our understanding of the universe and our place within it.

In the end, the UFO phenomenon is not just about the possibility of extraterrestrial life—it's about our own humanity. It's about our desire to understand the unknown, to explore the mysteries of the cosmos, and to find our place in a vast and complex universe. As we continue this journey, we must remember that the quest for knowledge is not just about discovering what lies beyond the stars —it's about discovering what lies within ourselves.

Epilogue: The Final Frontier

As we reach the end of our journey through the mysteries of alien encounters and the search for extraterrestrial life, it's clear that this is only the beginning. The questions we've explored in this book are far from being fully answered. Instead, they serve as a starting point for a deeper exploration of the universe and our place within it. Whether or not we are alone in the cosmos remains one of the greatest mysteries of our time, and the search for the truth continues to drive scientists, researchers, and curious minds around the world.

The possibility of contact with extraterrestrial beings challenges us to think beyond the limits of our current knowledge, to imagine new possibilities, and to prepare for a future that might look very different from the present. It invites us to embrace the unknown with courage and curiosity, to approach the mysteries of the universe with an open mind, and to recognize that our journey is far from over.

As we look to the stars, we must also look within ourselves, asking what it means to be human in a universe that might be teeming with life. The answers we find—or don't find—will shape the future of our species and our planet.

Whatever the future holds, one thing is certain: the quest to understand our place in the universe is a journey that will continue for generations to come. And it is a journey that we are all a part of.

End Word by the Author

Writing this book has been an extraordinary journey, one that has taken me from the ancient myths of distant cultures to the cutting-edge science of modern astronomy. Along the way, I've encountered stories that have both inspired and unsettled me, and I've had the privilege of exploring some of the most profound questions that humanity has ever faced.

This book is not just a collection of facts and theories—it's a reflection of my own curiosity and my desire to understand the world we live in. I hope that as you've read these pages, you've felt a similar sense of wonder and discovery. The possibility of extraterrestrial life is one of the most fascinating and challenging topics we can explore, and I'm grateful for the opportunity to share this exploration with you.

I want to express my deepest gratitude to my readers. Your interest in these topics keeps the conversation alive and pushes the boundaries of what we know. Whether you're a sceptic, a believer, or simply curious, I hope this book has given you new insights and sparked new questions.

As we move forward into the future, I encourage you to keep asking questions, to keep exploring, and to never lose your sense of wonder. The universe is vast and mysterious, and there is still so much to learn. Together, we can continue the journey of discovery and push the limits of our understanding.

About the Author

Emma is a writer, researcher, and lifelong explorer of the unknown. Fascinated by the mysteries of the universe from a young age, Emma has spent years studying the history, science, and culture of extraterrestrial encounters. Her work is driven by a deep curiosity about the cosmos and a passion for uncovering the truths that lie beyond the stars.

Emma's writing reflects her belief that the search for extraterrestrial life is not just a scientific endeavour, but a human one—an exploration that challenges our understanding of reality and our place in the universe. Through her books, articles, and talks, Emma seeks to inspire others to look beyond the horizon and to approach the unknown with an open mind and a sense of wonder.

When she's not writing, Emma enjoys stargazing, traveling to ancient sites, and discussing the mysteries of the universe with her husband, Harry.

Appendices

Appendix A: Glossary of Key Terms

- **UFO (Unidentified Flying Object):** A term used to describe any airborne object that cannot be immediately identified. Often associated with sightings of potential extraterrestrial craft.

- **UAP (Unidentified Aerial Phenomenon):** The modern term used by governments and researchers to describe unexplained aerial phenomena, replacing "UFO" to avoid the stigma associated with the term.

- **SETI (Search for Extraterrestrial Intelligence):** A scientific effort to detect signs of intelligent extraterrestrial life, primarily through the monitoring of radio signals from space.

- **Exoplanet:** A planet that orbits a star outside our solar system. The discovery of exoplanets has opened new possibilities for finding habitable worlds.

- **Fermi Paradox:** The apparent contradiction between the high probability of extraterrestrial civilizations existing in the galaxy and the lack of evidence for or contact with them.

- **Drake Equation:** A formula used to estimate the number of active, communicative extraterrestrial civilizations in the Milky Way galaxy.

- **Abduction Phenomenon:** Reports of individuals being taken against their will by non-human beings, often associated with invasive medical procedures and telepathic communication.

- **Project Blue Book:** A U.S. Air Force program that investigated UFO reports from 1952 to 1969, concluding that most sightings were misidentified natural or man-made phenomena.

- **Area 51:** A highly classified U.S. Air Force facility in Nevada, often associated with conspiracy theories about alien technology and government cover-ups.

Appendix B: Notable UFO Sightings and Abduction Cases

1. **Roswell Incident (1947):** A reported crash of an unidentified object near Roswell, New Mexico, which became a focal point for UFO and alien conspiracy theories.

2. **Betty and Barney Hill Abduction (1961):** The first widely publicized alien abduction case, involving a New Hampshire couple who claimed to have been taken aboard a UFO.

3. **Rendlesham Forest Incident (1980):** A series of sightings by U.S. military personnel in Suffolk, England, often referred to as "Britain's Roswell."

4. **Phoenix Lights (1997):** A mass sighting of a V-shaped formation of lights over Phoenix, Arizona, witnessed by thousands of people, including the state's governor.

5. **Travis Walton Abduction (1975):** A logger in Arizona who claimed to have been abducted by a UFO, inspiring the film *Fire in the Sky*.

Appendix C: Scientific Organizations and Resources

- **SETI Institute:** A leading organization in the search for extraterrestrial intelligence, conducting research and outreach programs.

- **MUFON (Mutual UFO Network):** A nonprofit organization dedicated to the scientific study of UFOs, collecting and analyzing reports from the public.

- **NASA Exoplanet Exploration:** NASA's program focused on the search for exoplanets and understanding their potential for supporting life.

- **Center for UFO Studies (CUFOS):** A scientific

organization founded by astronomer J. Allen Hynek, dedicated to the investigation of UFO phenomena.

Bibliography

Books and Articles

- Aubeck, Chris, and Jacques Vallée. *Wonders in the Sky: Unexplained Aerial Objects from Antiquity to Modern Times.* New York: TarcherPerigee, 2010.

- Drake, Frank. *The Drake Equation: Estimating the Odds of Intelligent Life Out There.* Cambridge: Cambridge University Press, 1984.

- Friedman, Stanton T. *Flying Saucers and Science: A Scientist Investigates the Mysteries of UFOs.* New Page Books, 2008.

- Greer, Steven M. *Unacknowledged: An Exposé of the World's Greatest Secret.* New York: Hay House, 2017.

- Jacobs, David M. *The Threat: Revealing the Secret Alien Agenda.* New York: Simon & Schuster, 1998.

- Kean, Leslie. *UFOs: Generals, Pilots, and Government Officials Go on the Record.* New York: Crown Publishing, 2010.

- Lazar, Bob, and George Knapp. *Dreamland: An Autobiography.* Los Angeles: Interstellar, 2019.

- Mack, John E. *Abduction: Human Encounters with Aliens.* New York: Scribner, 1994.

- von Däniken, Erich. *Chariots of the Gods? Unsolved Mysteries of the Past.* New York: Berkley Publishing Group, 1968.

Documentaries and Media

- *Close Encounters of the Third Kind.* Directed by Steven Spielberg, Columbia Pictures, 1977.

- *The Phenomenon.* Directed by James Fox, 1091 Media,

2020.

- *Unacknowledged: An Exposé of the World's Greatest Secret.* Directed by Michael Mazzola, A Sirius Disclosure Production, 2017.

- *Ancient Aliens.* History Channel, 2009-present.

- *Fire in the Sky.* Directed by Robert Lieberman, Paramount Pictures, 1993.

Government Documents and Reports

- U.S. Department of Defence. *Unidentified Aerial Phenomena Task Force Report.* Washington, D.C.: Office of the Director of National Intelligence, 2021.

- U.S. Air Force. *Project Blue Book: The U.S. Air Force's UFO Investigations.* Government Printing Office, 1969.

- Brazilian Air Force. *Operação Prato (Operation Saucer) Report.* Brasília: Brazilian Ministry of Defence, 1980.

www.ingramcontent.com/pod-product-compliance
Lightning Source LLC
Chambersburg PA
CBHW050747250726
48662CB00005B/2063